P9-DYD-765

626391

Take-Along Guide

Tracks, Scats and Signs

by Leslie Dendy
illustrations by Linda Garrow

ANACORTES PUBLIC LIBRARY
ANACORTES, WA 98221

NorthWord Press
Minnetonka, Minnesota

© Leslie Dendy, 1995

NorthWord Press
5900 Green Oak Drive
Minnetonka, MN 55343
1-800-328-3895

All rights reserved. No part of this work covered by the copyrights hereon may be reproduced or used in any form or by any means—graphic, electronic or mechanical, including photocopying, recording, taping of information on storage and retrieval systems—without the prior written permission of the publisher.

Illustrations by Linda Garrow
Book design by Lisa Moore

Library of Congress Cataloging-in-Publication Data

Dendy, Leslie A.
    Tracks, scats, and signs / by Leslie A. Dendy ; illustrations by Linda Garrow.
        p.   cm.
    ISBN 1-55971-481-6
    1. Animal tracks—Juvenile literature. 2. Animal tracks—Identification—Juvenile literature. [1. Animal tracks. 2. Animals—Habits and behavior.]
I. Garrow, Linda, ill.
    II. Title.
    QL768.D46   1995
    596—dc20   95-6207

Printed in Malaysia

DEDICATION

To my father, the scientist, whose curiosity is still contagious. And to my mother, the artist, who saw beauty in every blossom and beaver.

ACKNOWLEDGMENTS

Much of the information in this book is based on the expert knowledge of wildlife scientists with lifetimes of tracking experience. The adult tracking books of Olaus J. Murie, Paul Rezendes, Chris Stall, Louise Richardson Forrest, and Preben Bang are highly recommended to anyone who gets hooked on tracking and wants to learn more.

I would also like to thank my husband and children for their help and encouragement on my own fact-finding field trips. Blair and Laura Swartz generously donated bear scat and squirrel nibblings from their yard.

The library staff at University of New Mexico-Los Alamos provided a never-ending stream of interlibrary loan materials and enthusiasm. And Barbara Harold at NorthWord Press helped me see the forest through all the trees.

CONTENTS

INTRODUCTION --------------------- 6
BE SMART AND SAFE ---------------- 9

THE FOREST ----------------------- 10
  RABBITS ----------------------- 11
  WOODPECKERS ------------------- 12
  SQUIRRELS --------------------- 14
  PORCUPINES -------------------- 15
  DEER -------------------------- 16
VISIT A ROTTEN LOG HOTEL --------- 18

THE FIELD ------------------------ 20
  FOXES ------------------------- 21
  SKUNKS ------------------------ 22
  COYOTES ----------------------- 23
  SNAKES ------------------------ 24
  BADGERS ----------------------- 26
WALK LIKE THE ANIMALS ------------ 27

THE POND ------------------------- 28
  DUCKS ------------------------- 29
  RACCOONS ---------------------- 30
  MINKS ------------------------- 32
  MUSKRATS ---------------------- 34
  TURTLES ----------------------- 35
  FROGS ------------------------- 36
  BEAVERS ----------------------- 38
MAKE TRACKS THAT LAST ------------ 40

SCRAPBOOK ------------------------ 42

INTRODUCTION

There are many wild animals in fields and forests and ponds. Some of them are easy to see. But a lot of them are hard to find.

Wild animals leave clues everywhere they go. They dig underground tunnels. They make footprints in snow or mud. They chew plants along the way, and poop in their paths. They build nests. Their feathers and fur and dried skins fall off.

Be careful when you look for clues. Many of them blend in with the ground and the plants. You can bring a pencil and use the blank pages at the back of this book to draw what you see. A magnifying glass is fun to bring along also. You can use the ruler on the back of this book to measure what you find. The more time you spend looking for them, the more clues you will discover.

TRACKS

Animal footprints are called tracks. It's easy to find tracks in the snow. You can also find them in soft or muddy places when you walk along a path or dirt road. Look at the mud along the edges of streams, rivers, and ponds. Look in the sand at the beach, too.

Hunt for tracks that show clear toe prints. Count the toes and look at their shapes. Look for tiny dots made by the animal's claws.

Be sure to notice the size of the tracks. Squirrels and raccoons both make tracks that look like little hands, but raccoon tracks are two or three times bigger.

SCATS

Dogs poop on lawns, and people hurry to clean it up. Wild animal poop is another story. It even tells a story—about which animal came by and what it had eaten.

Scientists call the poop "scat." They call small pieces "droppings" or "scats." Scats come in many shapes and sizes. Most of them are not stinky.

Scats contain pieces of food that the animal could not digest. Rabbit droppings contain tiny pieces of twigs and leaves. Skunk scat is packed with insect bodies and wings. Fox scat may be full of mouse fur and bones one day, and blueberry or apple skins another day.

Look for scat near an animal's tracks or near its nest. You can use a stick to break it apart to see what is in it.

SIGNS

Wild animals leave many other clues about their busy lives besides tracks and scats. All the clues are called signs. A sign is anything you see that tells you where an animal has been and what it was doing. When an owl eats mice, moles, or voles, it digests the meat. Then it spits up a hard brown blob called a "pellet." It's full of fur and tiny bones and skulls.

Spiders let out liquid silk, which hardens into shiny threads. They use some threads as safety lines, like a rock climber's ropes. They also make webs to catch insects. Then they wrap some insects in tiny silk packages before they bite them.

A bird has thousands of feathers, and they fall off sometimes so new ones can grow. If you find a big pile of feathers, the bird was probably killed by a cat or a hawk. Or you can look for bird droppings on leaves.

Some wasps chew wood into tiny pieces to make paper. They build a tiny paper room for each baby, and wrap more paper around the outside.

These are just some of the signs you can look for to help identify which animals have been in the area.

BE SMART AND SAFE

Woods and other wild places are great fun, but they are wild. You probably won't be chased by a bear, but you could get bitten by a tick or a snake if you are not careful. You could get sunburned or bump into poison ivy. Always go with a grownup who knows the dangers in your area.

Here are three rules that wildlife scientists use to stay safe:

1 Don't touch wild animals. They are normally shy and afraid of people. If a wild animal lets you get close, it is probably sick or injured. It could bite. Leave it alone and call the animal experts. Also, never touch baby animals or birds. Just because you do not see the parents nearby does not mean the babies are alone. Touching them may make the parents angry and dangerous.

2 Don't eat wild plants or berries, unless a plant expert tells you it will not hurt you.

3 Don't touch animal nests or scats with your bare hands. They may contain bacteria, fleas, or other pests that could make you sick.

THE FOREST

For the animals that live in a forest, the trees and bushes are not just scenery. They are houses and food. Animals drill holes in the trunk or build nests in the branches. They gobble leaves, fruits, and nuts. They bite off the bark. They even eat the dead leaves and pine needles on the ground.

Look at the plants from top to bottom. You might see bear claw marks marching up a tree trunk. Down below, snails and slugs make their own slippery, slimy sidewalks across leaves and logs.

Leaves are like lettuce for caterpillars and grasshoppers, grubs, and slugs. Some chew big holes or tiny tunnels. Others suck the sugary leaf juice and make the leaves shrivel. Many butterflies, moths, and bugs hide their tiny, bead-like eggs on the bottoms of leaves. Then the hungry birds won't find them. But you can when you know what to look for!

RABBITS

Rabbits hop around hunting for plants to eat. And they hop in a hurry to escape enemies like owls and foxes.

Rabbit tracks are especially easy to see in the snow. When a rabbit hops, its four feet land in a clump shaped like a Y or a V.

Rabbit scats are hard balls, the size of peas or marbles. If you find a lot, the rabbit probably stopped there to eat. Look for branches that were bitten off with a diagonal cut.

A rabbit nest is like a bowl in the ground. It may be hidden under a bush. When a mother has babies, she puts grass and some of her fur inside the nest for them.

WOODPECKERS

What pecks all those holes in tree trunks? Woodpeckers, of course.

Hidden under the tree bark, many beetles and ants are chewing tunnels in the wood and laying their eggs. Woodpeckers can hear the insects chewing.

A woodpecker hammers its beak into the bark to make a hole. Its long tongue reaches through the tunnels and—zap!—grabs a snack.

Woodpeckers make bigger holes for nests.
The mother bird puts small wood chips in the hole, and
lays her eggs on them.

Many other animals borrow woodpecker holes
later. If you find one, it could have squirrels or owls or
raccoons inside.

SQUIRRELS

Squirrels leave their lunch leftovers on the ground. They drop empty acorns near oak trees. They chomp holes in hickory nuts and leave the shells behind. They also tear apart pine cones to eat the tasty seeds hidden inside.

You may also find a pile of little branches under a tree. Squirrels bite off small branches, so they can get the pine cones or tender buds at the end. They drop the rest of the branch to the ground.

Some squirrels make round nests as big as basketballs in the tree-tops. They build the nests with twigs, leaves, grass, or bark. Other squirrels live in old woodpecker holes.

Squirrel tracks look almost like doll hands. Look for them along a muddy road, or scampering across the snow from tree to tree.

PORCUPINES

A prickly porcupine can stab an enemy with its 30,000 quills. It doesn't need to run away fast. It waddles like a duck, and its tail drags on the ground. The quills make brush marks in the dust or snow.

When snow is deep, a porcupine just plows through, making a wavy ditch.

Porcupines climb trees to get tender twigs, buds, or acorns. They drop acorn shells and bitten-off branches under the tree. Some trees have huge bare spots where porcupines have pulled off the bark and eaten it.

Porcupine scats are shaped like peanuts or cashew nuts. They may be connected like a necklace.

DEER

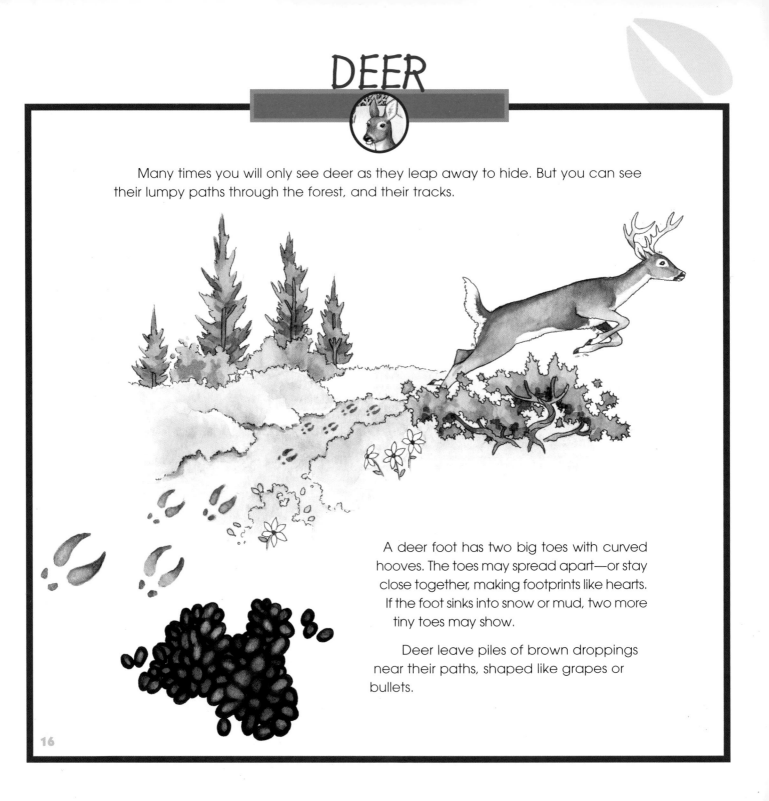

Many times you will only see deer as they leap away to hide. But you can see their lumpy paths through the forest, and their tracks.

A deer foot has two big toes with curved hooves. The toes may spread apart—or stay close together, making footprints like hearts. If the foot sinks into snow or mud, two more tiny toes may show.

Deer leave piles of brown droppings near their paths, shaped like grapes or bullets.

When a deer nibbles trees and shrubs, the chewed ends look rough. This is because a deer has no top front teeth. It rips a branch with its bottom teeth and lips. Deer also bite strips of bark off trees.

A deer "bed" is a mashed-down place in snow or grass, as big as a sled.

VISIT A ROTTEN LOG HOTEL

When a tree dies, it rots slowly. The wood gets softer. Animals dig and chew little "rooms" inside it, where they can stay safe and be warm in the winter. Even after they move out, you can see the signs they left behind.

It's fun to pick apart a rotten log or stump with a pocket knife or stick. You can make a list of the animals and signs you find, and you can draw them on the blank pages at the back of this book.

1 First kick the log gently, to scare away any snakes that may be hiding inside. If the log is damp, you may see slime trails of snails or slugs on it.

2 Peel off a strip of loose bark. There could be a caterpillar or salamander underneath. You may see tiny tunnels, chewed by beetles and ants.

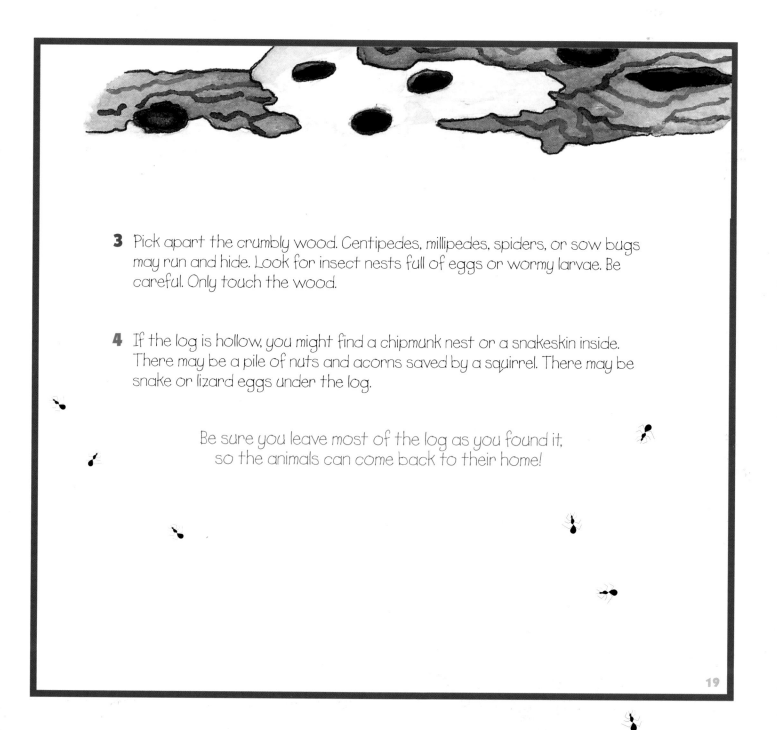

3 Pick apart the crumbly wood. Centipedes, millipedes, spiders, or sow bugs may run and hide. Look for insect nests full of eggs or wormy larvae. Be careful. Only touch the wood.

4 If the log is hollow, you might find a chipmunk nest or a snakeskin inside. There may be a pile of nuts and acorns saved by a squirrel. There may be snake or lizard eggs under the log.

Be sure you leave most of the log as you found it,
so the animals can come back to their home!

THE FIELD

Grasshoppers and butterflies are easy to find in a field, but many animals are hiding. Look for paths mashed down in the grass.

Hunt for little piles of dirt. These mounds could mark the "door" to the home of a dirt-digger, like a badger or a woodchuck.

Watch ants carrying food to their nest along tiny trails. The ants can smell their way. They make trails by dotting chemicals on the ground with their tail-ends.

Look closely at the plants. You may find a funnel-shaped spider web or a pile of grass pieces chewed by a mouse.

FOXES

Finding a fox is tricky business. But you can find fox tracks trotting through a field or forest.

A fox paw print has four toes with claw marks. A fox often walks in a straight line. Its rear feet step in the same spots as its front feet. This makes a neat dotted line. If you see sloppier tracks wandering around, they probably were made by a dog.

A fox family often lives in a burrow that was dug by a woodchuck or badger. The "front door" hole is as wide as a soccer ball. When the foxes kick dirt out of the den, it makes a big pile on one side. You may find fox leftovers on the pile, such as feathers, bones, or mouse fur.

SKUNKS

Your nose knows when a skunk is near. A skunk can squirt stinky spray in an enemy's face. The smell can tell you where to look for more signs—if you dare!

You might find the skunk's sleeping place. It could be a hole in the ground or under a building.

Skunk scat is dark and chunky. Poke it with a stick. It may be full of bee wings or plant seeds or mouse fur. And you can guess what the skunk was eating.

Skunks have long claws for digging up mouse and bee nests in the ground. You may find the holes where a skunk dug. And you can see little claw dots in their footprints.

COYOTES

If coyotes live nearby, you may be wakened by their howling songs and barks in the middle of the night.

Coyotes run long distances in fields or forests, often along human trails. In the snow, the tracks go on and on. They often make a straight dotted line, like fox tracks. A coyote paw print is oval with four toes and two middle claw dots. A rounder print with spread-apart toes could be a dog's print.

Coyote scats are the size of fat hot dogs. Like fox droppings, they may be full of fruit in the summer, or mouse hairs and bones in other seasons.

23

SNAKES

A snake can slide between the blades of grass and sneak up on a frog. It can slither into a mouse tunnel.

How can an animal with no feet make tracks?

Under the smooth, scaly skin are many muscles. The muscles push the snake's body against every little stone or blade of grass.

The snake's whole body slithers forward and makes a curvy track.

This is tough on the snake's skin. But it can grow a new skin every few months, inside the old skin.

When it's ready to shed, the snake rubs its head on a rock or branch to tear the old skin. Then it crawls around. The old skin is peeled off, inside out. You might find it on the ground.

BADGERS

Here's a great dirt-digger. A badger can dig faster than a human with a shovel. It tears many rough holes in the ground, hunting for mice or prairie dogs that live underground.

A badger also digs tunnels and underground rooms for its own home. The "front door" hole on top is big.

Badger tracks have five toes and claw dots—like a skunk's but bigger. Badger scat may be full of fur and little bones.

WALK LIKE THE ANIMALS

Groups of tracks are great clues. Try making different track patterns yourself on a snowy field—or a vacant lot, golf course, or football field. Take along a tape measure.

STRIDE

The distance between footprints is called the "stride." Walk slowly across the snow. Measure the distance between your tracks, from one toe tip to the next. Now try running. Your stride changed a lot—it got longer.

Stride is a clue about how big an animal is. A muskrat's stride is about 4 or 5 inches. A moose's stride may be 3 feet or more.

HOPPING

You can hop with two feet. Rabbits, squirrels, and mice hop with four feet. The front feet land first. Then the back feet come down in front of the front feet. Put your hands down and try to hop that way.

How far can you hop? A mouse usually hops a few inches. A jackrabbit can hop 10 feet or more.

TIGHTROPE WALKING

Foxes and coyotes often walk in a very straight line. Walk across the snow as if you were walking on a tightrope. Keep your tracks in one line.

Foxes and coyotes do this with four feet. The back feet step right on top of the front foot tracks. Bend over and walk on your hands and feet. Try to copy the straight line of fox and coyote tracks.

THE POND

A pond or lake is a natural gathering place. Some animals live in the water. Others visit the pond to drink the water and eat the pond plants and animals.

Look at the mud along the shore for tracks. Some trails may lead away from the pond into a forest or field nearby.

Look at the plants near the shore. They may have been nibbled by ducks or insects. There may be bird nests hidden in the reeds. Dried skeletons of dragonflies may be stuck to the stems. You may see frog or fish eggs in the shallow water.

DUCKS

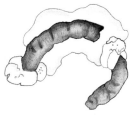

When a duck paddles across a pond, its webbed feet push the water like a diver's rubber flippers. When it walks on land, it waddles. You can see three straight toes in each footprint. You can often see the web of skin stretched between the toes.

A mother duck hides her nest in the reeds or grass at the edge of the pond. The nest is made of grass and some of her own soft down feathers. She lays her eggs there.

When the fluffy ducklings are strong enough to walk, they follow their mother to the water. Then you'll see big and little tracks together.

RACCOONS

The first raccoon sign you find may be garbage pulled out of a trash can.
Raccoons often visit campgrounds and houses. They eat almost anything.

They eat plenty of pond food, too, and leave their own "trash" as clues. They drop crayfish claws and empty turtle shells. They make holes in the ground when they dig up turtle eggs. They tear up duck nests and scatter the empty eggshell halves.

Raccoons walk many miles around ponds and rivers, summer and winter. The tracks look like little hands. A raccoon's front feet work like hands. Its quick fingers can catch fish or frogs or crayfish under water.

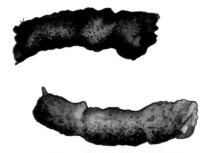

MINKS

If you smell a stink near water, think mink. This little hunter has a smell a bit different from a skunk's, but just as strong.

Minks make tracks along the edges of ponds, streams, and swamps. That's where they hunt for their meals. They eat muskrats, mice, fish, frogs, birds, worms, and insects.

Minks leave twisty, black scats on rocks and logs.

When it snows, minks play!

They slide down hills, sometimes right into an icy stream. The slide marks are as wide as your hand. They also dive into the snow, "swim" through it, and pop up several feet away. You may see the dive holes near their tracks.

MUSKRATS

When this fat rat runs around a pond, it makes hand-like footprints. Sometimes its skinny tail drags in the mud or snow, making curvy lines.

Muskrats pile up pond plants and sticks to make a lodge. Lodges are built out in a shallow pond or lake, or on the shore. Muskrats eat a lot of plants, and leave piles of plant stalks lying on the bank or on the water.

They munch clams and drop the clamshells. They leave peanut-size droppings on rocks or logs.

In the winter, muskrats make little huts for safe snacking. They collect plants and mud from the bottom of the pond. Next, they push it up through a hole in the ice, and make the roof for the hut. Then, they swim back under the ice to find food, and pop up into the hut to eat it.

TURTLES

If you see a straight stripe in the mud, with footprints on both sides, it's probably a turtle track. A turtle's stomach is close to the ground. If the shell drags on the ground, it makes a wide stripe. Sometimes only the tail drags, making a thin stripe.

In the summer a mother turtle lays her eggs in the ground. She digs a hole, lays the eggs inside, and covers them with dirt or sand. She may smooth the sand to hide the nest. Many raccoons, skunks, and bears can find it anyway, and eat the eggs. If you find a turtle nest, it's best to leave it alone.

35

FROGS

The long back legs of a frog are great for leaping.
When a frog is hopping across the mud, it lands
with four footprints in a clump—
two large and two small.

The big back feet are like swimming flippers.
The front feet are much smaller, with four tiny toes.

In the spring a female frog lays eggs in the water at the edge of the pond. Each black and white egg, about the size of a peppercorn, is wrapped in a clear jelly coat.

You may find thousands of eggs in a gooey blob, clinging to the pond plants. Later on, tadpoles with tails hatch out of the eggs, and swim in the pond.

BEAVERS

Using its front teeth, a beaver can chop down a tree in three minutes! Pointy-top tree stumps tell you a beaver pond is nearby.

Beavers can make their own ponds by building a dam across a stream with logs and mud. You can see trails where the beavers dragged logs. A wide zigzag in the mud shows where a beaver's fat tail was dragging.

Beavers also pile up sticks and mud to make their lodge. The "doors" are hidden under water.

When a beaver eats, it twirls a branch in its paws like corn on the cob. It gobbles the twigs, leaves, and bark. Then it weaves the bare branch into the dam or lodge.

Beavers keep busy all winter. You can see log-drag trails in the snow, or a pile of branches sticking out of the icy pond.

After many years the beavers move away. If the old dam breaks, the water rushes out. Then a meadow grows where the pond was. But you can still see the dam and lodge poking through the grass.

MAKE TRACKS THAT LAST

Animal tracks are just holes in the ground, but you can collect them with this trick. You can fill the tracks with liquid plaster, let it harden, and take the hard "casts" home. They look just like the bottoms of animal feet. This works best for tracks in mud or soft dirt.

HERE IS WHAT YOU WILL NEED

- plaster of Paris powder—in a plastic tub or coffee can with lid
- water—in a water bottle or canteen
- 1 cup measure for plaster powder
- 1/2 cup measure for water
- container to mix plaster in
- spoon
- pocket knife or table knife
- small box

HERE IS HOW TO MAKE THE PLASTER CASTS

1 Find some tracks first. Pick out two or three of the best ones.

2 Put 1/2 cup water in the mixing container.

3 Pour 1 cup plaster powder into the water.

4 Stir with the spoon until the lumps are gone. The plaster should be about as thick as pancake batter or applesauce.

5 QUICKLY pour the plaster into the tracks. Make sure it fills up all the toe holes and claw marks.

6 Let the plaster harden at least 20 to 40 minutes, until it feels as hard as a rock. Look around for more signs while you wait.

7 The casts are still fragile. Carefully cut the dirt around them with the knife, and lift them up gently.

8 Put the casts in the box to protect them on the way home. They will get harder after several hours. You can then rinse the dirt off in the sink. A soft toothbrush helps.

Tracks, Scats and Signs

44